Camper vans, ex-pats & Spanish hounds

**Tania Coates
& Sam Morris**

The strays of Spain: from road trip to rescue

Hubble & Hattie

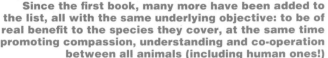

The Hubble & Hattie imprint was launched in 2009 and is named in memory of two very special Westie sisters owned by Veloce's proprietors.
Since the first book, many more have been added to the list, all with the same underlying objective: to be of real benefit to the species they cover, at the same time promoting compassion, understanding and co-operation between all animals (including human ones!)
Hubble & Hattie is the home of a range of books that cover all-things animal, produced to the same high quality of content and presentation as our motoring books, and offering the same great value for money.

More great titles from Hubble & Hattie

www.hubbleandhattie.com

Tania and Iyela

Wedding Day with very special guests of honour

First published in September 2013 by Veloce Publishing Limited, Veloce House, Parkway Farm Business Park, Middle Farm Way, Poundbury, Dorchester, Dorset, DT1 3AR, England. Fax 01305 250479/e-mail info@hubbleandhattie.com/web www.hubbleandhattie.com
ISBN: 978-1-845845-70-4 UPC: 6-36847-04570-8. © Tania Coates, Sam Morris & Veloce Publishing Ltd 2013. All rights reserved. With the exception of quoting brief passages for the purpose of review, no part of this publication may be recorded, reproduced or transmitted by any means, including photocopying, without the written permission of Veloce Publishing Ltd. Throughout this book logos, model names and designations, etc, have been used for the purposes of identification, illustration and decoration. Such names are the property of the trademark holder as this is not an official publication.
Readers with ideas for books about animals, or animal-related topics, are invited to write to the editorial director of Veloce Publishing at the above address. British Library Cataloguing in Publication Data – A catalogue record for this book is available from the British Library. Typesetting, design and page make-up all by Veloce Publishing Ltd on Apple Mac. Printed in India by Replika Press

Contents

Acknowledgements

Dedication
For Iyela and Zora

In no particular order I would like to thank the following people, without whom it would be impossible to undertake the work we currently do –

Sam for putting my experiences, thoughts and opinions into words. Nicky, Colin, Toby and Elliot Williams for their endless support: fostering, late night phone calls, and always being there for us – I have never met such caring, kind and unselfish people. Annie Dowell for her help and for suggesting that we should write this book. Tony Byford for all the amazing work he does and for founding SOS Animals in Spain. Therese Rantzow for her dedication and for answering my endless questions. Meg Sully for her wonderful help running the UK branch of SOS Animals. Pauline and Terry, whose lifestyle and dedication is a continuing source of inspiration. Kelly, Phil and family for making all this possible, and for housing a bedraggled mess (me) when I was searching for Pedro. Both Sam's and my parents for accommodating our unique ideals.

Too many vets to mention, but particularly Sheila, Goran, and Alastair Greenway in London; Anna Morales and the vets in Spain; The Royal Veterinary College and The University of Cambridge Queen's Veterinary Hospital (specifically Nick Bexfield BVetMed PhD, who helped with Zora and Micky). Tracy Van Der Murwe. Nicky and Greg Goldie for all their support and for adopting our first two foster dogs. Carol and Roy Talbot for their endless support.

My brother, Simon, and his wife, Kate, for deciding to get married in Spain. James Perry for all his help with our web site. Cathy Klar and her amazing family for their fundraising and support. All the volunteers who have worked, and are still working, at SOS Animals Spain and SOS Animals UK. Jude Brooks, and everyone at Hubble and Hattie for making this book possible.

Everyone who has fostered, adopted, home checked or helped with last-minute transport runs. All those who have helped transport the dogs from Spain, attended our fundraising events, walked a dog for us, donated, fund raised, supported our campaigns or followed us on Facebook and Twitter. My thanks will never be enough, but thank you: you all keep it going, and without you the dogs would not be saved.

Tania Coates

Foreword

A tiny trembling puppy apprehensively stared up at me from under the bins in a Torremolinos backstreet. She was frightened and hungry, and my first thought was: Oh God, what do I do now? Of course, this was a rhetorical question because there was no way I could walk away, but as I tucked her under my arm and headed home, I had no idea that deciding to rescue her would have such a huge impact on my life.

I'd moved to Spain in the mid-1990s. I was armed with a newly-acquired TEFL (Teaching English as a Foreign Language) certificate, and I planned to soak up the Spanish sun, experience the culture and enjoy a different pace of life, all washed down with a cold beer and financed by my plans to teach English to Spanish and other non-English speakers.

It had been a big step. Born in the Norfolk and Norwich Hospital, I grew up in rural Norfolk, part of a family that always had a dog: my mother was an animal-lover who passed that love onto me. Later, I found myself living and working in London, and when my company restructured I took the opportunity for redundancy. I'd enjoyed several holidays in Torremolinos, and decided the time was right to take the plunge; see if I could carve out a new life for myself.

Then little Giovanna came into my life, and it wasn't too long before I'd found a second puppy – what difference could one more make? I reasoned.

Hmmmm, how wrong can you be!

I met José, a Spaniard who also adored animals, and who lived nearby. Before long the two puppies became three, and then four, and José and I were able to support each other with caring for the dogs. But one Christmas I had to go to the UK and José had to go to Madrid, and so the search was on for someone to care for the dogs in our absence, which is how I came to know an English lady called Kim, who cared for people's animals and also did a little bit of rescue work. On my return we chatted about how sad the situation was in southern Spain regarding abandoned animals, and the seeds were sown ...

By mid-1997 we and two other animal-lovers had set up SOS (Spay our Strays), and by early 1999, had secured recognition as a registered charity. We pledged to help the abandoned and the abused, and find loving new homes whenever we could. Each dog was to be given care and affection, and, if need be, a secure, safe home with us, and since then SOS has helped literally thousands of animals.

Every cent we raised was used for our work, and we

never put to sleep a healthy animal. And our small charity grew and grew. It was different back then: there were only a couple of rescue organisations besides us, but an awful lot of abandoned and stray dogs. Many vets were operating solely as a business, and compassion did not seem to be at the top of their agenda, although there were, of course, exceptions.

Over the years some important changes in attitude have emerged, although there are still plenty of dogs wandering the streets and countryside. More people want to help – Spanish, English, and other nationalities, too – and nowadays the vast majority of vets want to help to make a difference, and are committed to spreading the word that neutering is the most sensible course of action to combat the problem. We have been privileged to work with some extraordinarily supportive vets who 'get' what we do and don't think we're mad!

And we are enormously privileged, too, to be supported in our work by our two sister charities: SOS in Sweden and SOS in the UK. For many years our Swedish colleagues have worked tirelessly to raise vital funds – we rely entirely on donations and what we can raise ourselves – and have supplied us with many young volunteers who pay their own fare and give their time freely for anything from a week to several months. They clean, feed, walk the dogs, help us with the regular vet visits, help care for animals who are sick, and do it all with huge enthusiasm. And it's not always youthful enthusiasm, either: our oldest volunteer is in her mid-sixties! Over the years many hundreds of our dogs have been found fabulous new homes in Sweden due to the hard-working efforts of the Swedish team.

It was an amazing series of events that brought SOS Spain to the attention of Tania and her husband, Sam. They were travelling through Spain on their way to a wedding in Antequera, inland from Malaga when, stopping for petrol on the outskirts of Madrid, they found a stray dog. There was no way that Tania was going to leave the dog behind, but he had to meet UK quarantine regulations before she could take him home. Tania tracked us down to see if we could help, and the link that was forged then has become stronger over the years. (By pure coincidence, I had grown up with Sam's mum in a village in Norfolk, and we had been great childhood friends.)

Tania has spread word of our work throughout the UK, and she and her small band work tirelessly to find fantastic homes for many of our dogs, including the very handsome Podenco hounds who can be real head turners but very difficult to rehome in Spain. And some of our older boys and girls have been given a new lease of life in caring forever homes in the UK.

Many years ago the problem of strays and abandoned dogs was often due to ignorance. Nowadays, the economic crisis plays a part, and whilst I know how difficult life has become for some, I am appalled by the 'Brits' who apparently find it easy to abandon their faithful four-legged friend – a member of the family – when they return to the UK, especially as we can help repatriate pets. It's upsettng and sad to find dogs abandoned in locked-up villas, tied to gates, or simply let loose in the countryside to fend for themselves.

Inevitably, our work can be very distressing, but this is more than made up for by the success stories, which this quote that I heard at an international animal conference exemplifies –

"It's better to light a candle than complain of the darkness."

I feel privileged to have helped light the SOS candle, and very proud and happy to have come to know so many wonderful people, who not only keep the candle burning, but ensure it burns brighter with each passing year.

Tony Byford
Founder of SOS Animals Spain

Introduction

Since establishing SOS Animals UK in 2008, Sam and I have found homes for around 400 dumped and stray dogs. We work with a group of dedicated volunteers in Spain who are inundated with dogs who have been abandoned by Spanish hunters and British expatriates. In 2010 we moved from London to a smallholding in Wales where we foster dogs prior to finding them their forever homes.

Much of the work we do is only made possible because of short-term fostering, which necessarily means that, as well as permanent homes, we also need many good foster homes. Fostering a dog can be emotionally difficult but also very rewarding, and will involve a rescue dog being taken into a home that will help him or her become used to life as a domestic pet. A fosterer can also help in the initial assessment of a dog's needs so that, ultimately, we can make the best match between dog and permanent home.

Whenever a possible forever home is found, our main concern at SOS UK is to match a dog's needs to the potential new owner. This will involve a detailed rehoming procedure that begins with discussion about the lifestyle, experience and expectations of the person who is interested in taking a dog, through to a home check and visit to see a dog at his or her new home.

We pride ourselves on ensuring that the home we find for each and every dog is the best possible for that animal, which can take a little time to achieve in some cases. The transition from stray to rescue, to foster dog, to much-loved companion is always our goal, and we concentrate on changing one animal's life at a time.

All of our work is undertaken by volunteers, so if you think you could help, or would like more information, please visit our website. www.sos-animals.org.uk.

Chapter one

Camper vans

We had a problem. Not a big problem in the grand scheme of things, but a problem nevertheless. In due course we would become well acquainted with what a real problem was – I suppose it's all a matter of perspective – but, with our entire family decamping to the south of Spain for my brother's wedding, who would care for our fifteen-year-old diabetic rescue dog, Iyela? I would not be happy having her stay in kennels, and my parents (her usual holiday hosts) would be off to Spain for the matrimonial celebrations.

Now, I quite accept that, in the eyes of some, this is not a life or death problem, but my husband, Sam, and I are true dog lovers, and we had been through so much with Iyela since I rescued her that there was no way I would be apart from her unless I was sure she was happy.

Luckily, a possible solution was thought of, and a quick phone call to the groom-to-be confirmed it: our little rescue dog would be going to Spain with us.

The plan was to drive down through France in Sam's Volkswagen camper van; head south over the Pyrenees, then across the Spanish plains to the wedding venue – a hotel in the south eastern foothills of the Sierra Nevada. Three days on the road would see us and our four-legged companion arrive bright-eyed and ready for the celebrations.

It all sounded so simple in conversation, and not even that taxing when put to paper. How naïve we were ...

Sam relished the pre-departure preparations, and even found time to change the complete exhaust on the camper: rust-spotted bits of metal came off with only a little persuasion, to be replaced by shiny stainless steel. With pet passport, a loaded roof rack, and a fridge full of canine insulin, we set off south.

A morning train took us through the Euro tunnel, and we chose the more westerly route to avoid Paris, heading through the old Norman capital of Rouen. Passing its gothic cathedral and driving over the River Seine, we motored steadily on into the Pays de la Loire region of France. Completing our first day's drive – a gentle trek of around 370 miles (595km) – we stopped for the night in a small rural camp site just north of Le Mans.

The weather had been clear and mild, and the journey so far great fun. The irony of chugging along in the Volkswagen so near the legendary racetrack of Le Mans was not lost on us. The air-cooled engine of the camper makes a wonderfully unique sound, so distinctive of Volkswagens of that period – somewhere between a steam engine, a biplane, and an old lawn mower – the chugging a reassuring soundtrack to our journey.

That evening we bought beer and fresh bread from

With pet passport, a loaded roof rack on our 'greenhouse on wheels,' and a fridge full of canine insulin, we set off south.

the boulangerie in the local village, cooked dinner on our camping stove using some vegetables we had picked from our allotment, and enjoyed the seclusion of the off-season camp site in a slightly obscure location in France.

The next morning we continued south, leaving Le Mans and driving out of the Pays de la Loire through Poitou Charentes and on into Aquitaine, where the scenery turned from distinctly northern European to more Mediterranean. Northern France has a recognisable quality if you have ever lived in the south east of England: gently undulating, fertile and well-watered agricultural vistas, similar to those found in Sussex or Kent, took on a baked and heated southern European flavour. The stretch south from La Rochelle and past Bordeaux which runs parallel to the Atlantic coast felt sandblasted and windswept; the tough, pale green grasses and odd-shaped conifers reminiscent of southern Spain.

15

Left: Fuel and coffee stop in northern France ...

Above: ... and pitched-up for the night at a small rural campsite just north of Le Mans.

Iyela relaxing at the campsite, making herself at home.

Dinner that evening included onions and other vegetables from our London allotment.

A distinctly alpine feel.

vehicles which seem to separate the two dimensions. The counterpoint to this, of course, is that in hot weather, or when stationary, the interior rapidly heats up, just as a greenhouse would, and air conditioning was a somewhat late addition to Volkswagens – some twenty years late!

We decided to try and make up some mileage with the aim of getting to the wedding venue a day early to – hopefully – allow us some time to sit and sizzle by the pool. Driving through the day and on into the night, we pulled into a service station at about midnight and crashed out in the back of the camper. No quaint little French camp site tonight: this was a noisy truck stop beside a dusty road. We had covered around six hundred miles and were somewhere south of Burgos.

Pedro

On our third morning we headed towards Madrid, circumnavigating the city via metropolitan/suburban bypasses to reach the desolate Spanish plains. This was La Mancha, Don Quixote country, and, to a blinkered English eye used to greenery, it was vast agricultural emptiness. We paused for a late morning fuel and coffee stop at a service station about twenty kilometres (12 miles) south of Toledo. I often wonder how different things might have been if we had not stopped at this particular service station. The quirks of circumstance are funny things that take us in directions of

La Mancha: Don Quixote country; a harsh and arid landscape.

Approaching the border the landscape morphed from low-lying scrub to a distinctly alpine environment as we drove nearer to the Pyrenees. Goodbye France; hello Spain.

The drive through the Pyrenees was sublime, partly due to a diversion on the motorway which forced us onto an old route that snaked over hills like a piece of ribbon. Heavy cumulus clouds hung in the air and erupted as we descended into Spain, filling the sky with fork and sheet lightning, providing us with a truly spectacular pyrotechnic-like display.

One of the many beauties of travelling in an old Volkswagen camper is the panoramic view that can be had from all of the windows: a veritable greenhouse on wheels that allows total immersion in the landscape, unlike modern

which we have no knowledge: surely one of the wonders of chance and fate, as foresight may cause us to question the route we are taking.

While filling up with petrol we noticed a very skinny dog curled around the adjacent petrol pump, barely flinching as cars pulled into the service station; apparently asleep. He was all ribcage and head; so slim I could encircle his waist with my hands. At first we were unsure about approaching him, but when we took Iyela for a walk he got up and wandered after us, giving her a real good sniff, followed by a little gyration and a slight air-humping motion. Iyela was smitten, playing and encouraging him with licks around his mouth. He was a medium-to-large size Mastiff mix, with a head similar to that of a Great Dane, balanced on a chunky Labrador body.

We put Iyela back in the camper and went inside to pay for the petrol. The dog was wandering through the traffic as cars pulled in and out of the service station; it was only a matter of time before he was hit. We asked in the service station if anyone knew the owner. No one did. The staff sort of chuckled to themselves and told us that the dog had been there for a couple of days, and it was "Okay, the pound will collect him and he will be killed." We were shocked, but what could we do?

Back outside I put the dog on a lead and walked him away from the road, taking him around the petrol station to see if anyone would come forward to claim him, but the only response was people shooing him away.

A Spanish couple from Madrid could see our concern, and urged us to take him. I remembered that Sam's mum had mentioned a friend who had moved to southern Spain to start an animal shelter many years back. We thought that at least we could try and get him there, or to a vet to determine if he was microchipped.

We called Sam's mum who found the shelter details and gave us the phone number of SOS Animals Spain. A volunteer there told us they could possibly find a foster home for the stray in Antequera, where the wedding was taking place. Before leaving the area, however, we thought we should take him to a local vet to be scanned, just in case his owner could be identified and located in this way. If not, well, then it appeared we would be one extra on the journey south ...

Taking a bit of a gamble we left the service station with one extra dog, who got into our camper with

Pedro: our new travelling companion.

18

surprisingly little persuasion, leaving our contact details with the petrol station staff in case anyone came looking for him (the staff took the details reluctantly, giving the impression they felt this was a bit pointless). With a distinct lack of inspiration we tentatively named our new co-traveller Pedro. (Sam was quite keen on the name Jesús but I put my foot down.) Pedro seemed a little confused by the whole driving experience, and sat on the front seat facing backward. It was very difficult to try and get him to settle, but he seemed a gentle and calm character; Iyela liked him, which I felt was the most important thing. We found a small veterinary practice in the next town which could find no microchip in Pedro: it looked like he was staying with us.

Pedro and the three of us spent that night at a camp site just north of the Sierra Nevada range, some three hundred and thirty miles (530km) south of where we had started that day's journey, and around one hundred and sixty miles (257km) south of where Pedro had begun his day. Although obviously unsettled by his adventure, Pedro appeared to be coping quite well with the change in location and company. He would not eat any of the food we offered him on the journey, despite his semi-emaciated condition, and only when we tried him with a bowl of Iyela's special chicken soup did he eat.

That evening at the camp site we met an English couple who had just moved to Spain to open a gym, and they had a lovely Volkswagen camper in the baby blue and orange livery of the Gulf Racing team. Pedro greeted them and sat patiently with Iyela while we chatted. In the back of their camper was their pet parrot who had travelled with them from England. We were told that he could speak, but he was maybe a little bashful or tired after the journey as he stayed quiet. It was incredibly hot and muggy – there was not a breath of wind and it was uncomfortably sticky – even though still early evening, and I sympathised with how he felt.

That night Sam ended up sleeping outside on the ground, as Pedro could not settle in the van, his persistent moans and grumbles letting us know that he wanted out. Attaching a long lead to Pedro, Sam settled down with this wrapped around his waist. Neither of them slept much, however, as Pedro barked at every noise (and there was quite a bit of nocturnal activity on the site), each time leaping up and striding about, which, of course, tugged the lead wrapped around Sam's torso, jerking him sideways.

Pedro relaxing at the campsite, apparently without a care in the world!

Fellow-campers.

I got up early and took Iyela and Pedro for a wander in the surrounding countryside, leaving Sam to sleep in the camper van, which he never argues with, and especially not after the night he'd had. The land around the camp site was like a nature reserve – wild yet manicured, with paths leading off in all directions. It was stunning, but I was too jaded from the journey and worried about our hitchhiker to really appreciate it.

Pedro walked well on the lead, even better than Iyela, who had her own agenda at times. Around Pedro's neck was a heat-sealed plastic strip, of the type found around packages, which had clearly been intended to act as a rudimentary collar. When the three of us got back to Sam, who was now wide awake, I got him to cut it off.

Exploring the fabulous countryside around the campsite.

We set off in the camper into the Sierra Nevada range, but had a long, midday pit stop at a dusty service station as it was just too hot to travel during that time of day. The Volkswagen was doing its best greenhouse impression. Opening all the windows made little difference, and the feeble plug-in fans we had brought with us only circulated warm air around the interior.

Packing up before heading south to the Sierra Nevada with Pedro and Iyela.

We stayed parked in the shade for some two-and-a-half hours, all of the windows and doors wide open, but it was still oven-hot, and there was no wind. Large Spanish families spread rugs and blankets on the ground in the shade beside their cars, then slowly worked their way through a leisurely lunch, after which their children slept, draped this way and that across their cross-legged parents. The Spanish tradition of a midday siesta is something I could quite easily get used to!

Once it had finally cooled in late afternoon, we set out on the last leg, the four of us arriving at the wedding hotel looking a little post-camping scruffy. Our families were not at all surprised to discover that we had set off with one dog and now had two (they know us very well).

The wedding went well as weddings generally do, with Pedro and Iyela spending much of the day in the hotel bedroom. Although a little concerned about leaving them together unattended for so long, each time I checked on them I was greeted by wagging tails and licks. At every opportunity I took them out for walks and sat with them.

SOS Animals Spain

The day after the ceremony we took Pedro to the shelter, at that time located near Fuengirola on the Costa del Sol. SOS Animals Spain was established in 1997 by British expatriates who were appalled by the overwhelming population of stray cats and dogs around the south coast of Spain. By a complete quirk of chance, one of these ex-pats – Tony Byford – grew up with my mother-in-law in England.

Initially intended to cater for some fifty dogs, the shelter was well over capacity with about two hundred canines in residence, as the volunteers and rescuers never turn away a dog in need (and there are quite a few dogs in need).

We learned that the work done by SOS Spain is a very small part of a far bigger picture of animal suffering – the small but heartfelt attempt of a few individuals to chip

continued page 24

Overleaf: SOS Animals Spain and some of its residents.

away at the animal welfare problem in southern Spain – and that the huge number of dogs dumped by the supposedly animal-loving British had contributed considerably to the difficulty. The economic downturn had hit hard, and folk were packing up their villas, waving goodbye to the dream, and returning to the UK, dumping their dogs at the shelter or, worse, abandoning them, tethered to the front of their villas. We were appalled to hear of cases where canine remains had been found inside locked villas after the residents had left.

We quickly realised that taking Pedro to the shelter was not a solution to his plight; nor did it help the shelter. Sam and I felt pretty sure we could do whatever was necessary to get Pedro back home with us, although, for the six months required to get him a pet passport, he would have to stay at the shelter.

We now had the agonising ordeal of leaving Pedro and heading north. We had really bonded with him during our four days together: as mentioned, Pedro and Iyela had stayed in the hotel bedroom throughout the wedding, happily welcoming those who came in to see them. The pair of them sat beside our table at breakfast, sunbathing, the morning that we dropped off Pedro at the shelter. I could not wait until the two of them could be reunited.

Homeward bound

The return leg was not as eventful as our journey south, though we still managed to break down in northern Spain when a push rod gave out in the engine (or so Sam tells me). While the camper was being repaired in the local garage, we spent a night in Lizartza.

Lizartza sits in the province of Gipuzkoa – or Guipúzcoa, depending on whether you are of Basque or Spanish political persuasion – and by complete chance is one of the political strongholds of the armed Basque nationalist group ETA. It is so unanimously anti-Spain that when a non-elected, Madrid-supported mayor was imposed on the area, he had to be shepherded in under armed guard just to reach the town hall! Plastered throughout Lizartza's main square were images of imprisoned political prisoners, accompanied by ETA flags hanging from most houses and balconies. Despite this, it was a stunning location brimming with alpine village atmosphere. Most buildings had shallow-pitched roofs to cope with snow, and the crisp scent of the conifers and pine trees covering the steep hills filled the

Images of political prisoners at Lizartza.

air. Pumpkins, sweetcorn and runner beans grew in steeply sloped gardens, and the roads were devoid of traffic. For once, being English seemed to hold no political or historical stigma as ETA's contention is mainly with its own people, and French government to a degree.

We had a light meal and something to drink in a rustic bar where the locals (all very Basque with little English) wheeled out a British ex-pat called Mick, who was anywhere in age from mid-forties to mid-sixties, covered in tattoos of mixed Merchant Navy and prison origin, and sporting a serious, full-faced ginger beard. I romanticised that this must be a wonderfully secret spot for a rogue Brit who needed some anonymity to disappear in.

The drive back through France was uneventful; the miles filled with thoughts of Pedro and talk about what to do. Iyela sprawled out and slept on the back seat of the camper, and it was a relief to return to a milder climate as we left the channel tunnel and drove through Kent. As we chugged along the M20 motorway towards home, the VW's air-cooled engine decided it had finally had enough and gave up the ghost. We just managed to pull into a service station, two hours from home. Sadly, all of Sam's roadside tinkering, and later efforts of the breakdown man, were to no avail.

And so the last leg of our momentous journey was made via taxi while the Volkswagen was recovered to the garage that usually looked after it: not the most auspicious end to our journey.

As we slowly settled back into the hectic routine of life in London, the main thing on my mind was Pedro.

Chapter two

Ex-pats

I have been involved with animal rescue since an early age. During my gap year before I went to university I spent time in Eilat, Israel, where I kept finding stray dogs wandering the streets. This led me to a local animal shelter called Eilat Loves Animals, where, over a two-year period, I spent much of my time, eventually bringing two dogs home to England (their story would make a sizeable book in itself – one for the future, maybe).

Iyela and Zora spent six months in quarantine which was, in my opinion, the best way to spend my student loan. Zora passed away when she was eleven as a result of myeloma and Iyela – who travelled to Spain with us – passed away on New Year's Day 2011 at the age of seventeen. They are both sorely missed but I know that the life they so enjoyed would not have been possible had I not rescued them from the shelter in Eilat. This was one of the most worthwhile and satisfying things I have ever done, and I simply cannot put into words how much the pair meant to me. Vitally, the work we do now with regard to dog rescue would not have come about had it not been for these two amazing dogs.

Zora and Iyela.

Pedro's progress

Back in England after the trip through Spain, and with animal rescue now firmly flowing in my blood, I kept in close contact with SOS Animals Spain. Pedro had been paired up with a German Shepherd cross called Adrian, who had been dumped by expatriates, and we learnt that they were getting on very well together in a pen. Adrian – who we had briefly met when we left Pedro at the shelter – had been unsettled and not eating, and pairing up with Pedro was really helping him in these respects. I hinted to my husband that it would be a shame for them to be separated, and through careful prodding, cajoling and gentle persuasion, Sam eventually came round to the idea that, once Pedro had done his six-month stint at the shelter and acquired his pet passport, we would take both him and Adrian.

I felt slightly helpless at home in London, waiting while Pedro 'did his time,' so I began to collect old bedding and donated provisions to send out to the shelter in Spain, and generally drum up support for the work it does. Very soon I had received lots of collars, leads, beds, food and toys. It always amazes me what people will donate, and their generosity, if asked simply and honestly.

The situation with stray dogs and cats in Spain is unimaginably grim. There are always exceptions, of course, with everything, and there are those in the country – both Spanish and British – who love and care for their animals and pets. There is a strong hunting heritage in rural areas throughout Spain, and, generally, two breeds of dogs are traditionally used for hunting: the Galgo and the Podenco.

The Galgo

The Galgo is a sighthound, one of the ancient canine breeds, and is similar in appearance to a Greyhound (which is possibly a descendant of the Galgo). Both breeds have been crossed with each other in recent times, yet the Galgo is much hardier, with greater stamina for prolonged chases. The Galgo is a very fast hunter, but has not been bred exclusively for speed like the Greyhound, which can achieve and maintain forty-five miles an hour for a short period of time over a flat, even surface. A Galgo can reach around forty miles an hour on undulating surfaces, and maintain

The Galgo is a sighthound, one of the ancient dog breeds, commonly used for hunting hares in Spain.

Ex-hunting dogs at a Galgo sanctuary in southern Spain.

Estella, a rescued Galgo at SOS Animals Spain.

Main: A slender but tough body: built for both stamina and speed.

Inset: Galgos have the classic sighthound temperament: gentle, affectionate, loving.

this for prolonged periods. Physically, the Galgo is higher in the rear than in the front – characteristic of endurance runners – and has flatter muscling than the Greyhound.

Another feature that makes the breed suitable for hunting is its tough coat that, although thinner than that of some dogs, does not tear as easily as the Greyhound's, and can be either rough or smooth. Excelling at hunting hares in particular, the Galgo's slender looks have come about as a result of chasing this super-fast prey.

The name 'Galgo' probably has its origin in the Latin *Canis Gallicus* or 'dog from Gaul:' literally 'The Spanish dog.' The Gauls inhabited the Iberian Peninsula from around 400-600BC, and the breed probably derived from the dogs they took with them on their migration south.

Every year, the Campeonato de España de Galgos en Campo Copa de El Rey (Spanish Galgo Coursing Cup of Kings) is held near Toledo, a hunting and hare-coursing event whose lineage extends back through Spanish aristocracy. The unpolluted nature of the breed is a source of great pride – much as with the UK's Kennel Club – and the Galgo is, to a certain degree, considered a dog of the Spanish gentry. One of the most famous references to the Galgo is contained in the first lines of Miguel de Cervantes' *Don Quioxte*, and reflects how interwoven the breed is in the Spanish identity.

"In a village of La Mancha, the name of which I have no desire to call to mind, there lived not long since one of those gentlemen that keep a lance in the lance-rack, an old buckler, a lean hack, and a Galgo for coursing."

continued page 32

Right: A Galgo in rescue.

Overleaf: The breed is interwoven with Spanish culture and tradition.

The Podenco

The Podenco's story is very different, and to talk about breed, or even dog-type, is pointless because of fickle and subjective regional bickering at the Real Sociedad Canina España (Spanish Kennel Club); the inherent ridiculous nature of breed classification based on strict standards when dogs are bred for a specific job, and pure semantics.

The Podenco (which means 'hound' in Spanish) is primarily a multi-sensory canine, whose name applies to a vast number of dog types, dependent on quarry size and the region they come from. Climate and hunting habitat are primary motivators for determining their appearance but, generally, Podencos have similar proportions to Pharaoh Hounds, with long faces, pointy ears, large chests and legs built for speed (it's easier for a slim and long-legged dog to dissipate excess heat while hunting in the sun for long periods). Yet the variation in appearance across dog-type is huge, from the squat Podenco Maneto with his short legs (yes: short legs but still a Podenco!), best described as a Dachshund-like Podenco, and used to hunt in dense brush, to the large and regal Podenco Ibicenco (Ibizan Hound) used as a fast and agile hunter.

To further confuse matters some Podenco types can have variations but still retain the same generic name. An example of this is the Podenco Andaluz, with his three different sizes: talla grande, talla mediana, and talla chica. On top of this, all variations can have one of two coats: rough or smooth and tight. The rough-coated Podencos are sometimes called Griffin Podencos, which, although a rather wonderful name, doesn't make identification very easy.

As in other parts of Europe, these dogs are employed in various ways across the Spanish regions, the dog type and techniques used depending on prey, and whether or not the hunter has a gun. Animals as large as boar and deer are sometimes hunted with packs of dogs only, and for this the chunky and shaggy Podenco Campanero is generally the hound of choice (it's thought that a Podenco may have been bred with a Mastiff in order to achieve the heavier build required for larger game). Small game such as rabbits is often hunted with large packs of the small Podenco Maneto, and killed using both gun and dogs. The squat Maneto works by flushing the rabbits toward waiting guns (a technique familiar with other rural hunting communities across Europe).

continued page 37

A Podenco Andaluz in rescue.

The Podenco Andaluz is commonly seen throughout southern Spain.

Hopi, a deaf, rough-coated Andaluz, was rescued from the pound as a puppy.

The large Podenco Andaluz is sometimes used to hunt boar: here's one of our foster dogs 'hunting' a fluffy toy.

34

Left: The tough little Podenco Maneto is used to get into undergrowth and flush out prey.

A Podenco Andaluz deploying the characteristic 'Podenco jump.'

Penny and Gemma: a Podenco Ibicenco greeting.

An emaciated Galgo: sadly, an all-too-common sight ...

In the south it is very common for the large Podenco Ibicenco to be used in a similar way, except that the dog jumps over the low scrub, and nothing else is quite the same as a full, four-paws-in-the-air Podenco jump. Almost identical to a gazelle in strength and elegance, it's quite a sight to see any number of dogs in a large pack springing and leaping, and dashing off across a rocky slope. The landscape of southern Spain is a very unforgiving environment when it comes to hunting, which makes these feats of endurance and agility all the more impressive.

Tradition – not always a good thing

Hunting dogs, methods and lifestyle are woven into the very fabric and culture of rural Spain, and both the Podenco and the Galgo are generally regarded as hunting tools across the classes. In the worst cases the dogs live in very poor conditions, often starved prior to a hunt to make them keener. Dogs are generally selected for their utility and hunting skill, which can result in animals not considered up to standard being discarded, or used as breeding bitches. Sometimes, dogs as young as two are considered past their prime and summarily disposed of. The harsh reality is that dogs who cannot hunt to the expected level are an unnecessary and unwanted additional mouth to feed.

In Spain, unwanted dogs are abandoned, shot, drowned, hung or beaten to death. In some regions – and particularly poorer areas – as a bullet costs more than a length of rope, hanging is the method of choice. Unhappily, hanging is also a traditional method of killing unwanted dogs, passed down through generations of hunters. With the current economic climate hitting Spain hard, sadly, hanging as a method of disposal has become more common.

Some of the dogs who have been abandoned end up in Spanish pounds (perrera), generally very underfunded establishments with extremely dubious welfare standards. Dogs are often kept in very overcrowded, dirty pens, and many die (some expatriates refer to the perrera as 'killing stations'). Neutering in Spain is incredibly rare, and abandoned dogs breed uncontrollably, the resultant packs commonly seen loitering around dustbins or other locations where a source of food has been discovered. In

A chained Mastin Español at a finca in Spain: these dogs are commonly used to guard.

Being in a shelter can be very hard, and many dogs will be there their whole lives.

certain communities male castration is considered to be emasculating to both dog and owner, so dogs are left entire due to myth and ignorance.

Some hunters purchase new hounds at the beginning of the hunting season in September, and dispose of them at the end, as, unfortunately, it's cheaper to buy a new dog each season than it is to care for them until then.

When discussing the rescue work that we do – helping Spanish strays – a fairly commonly-heard remark is that 'the Spanish are so cruel,' the implication being that the British are not. Yet, the reality is that supposedly educated and caring British people are as guilty of cruelty and neglect as any Spaniard, and maybe even more so. Brits in general tend to feel that other countries are not as caring when it comes to animals – after all, are we not considered a nation of animal-lovers? – repeatedly citing bull fighting as an example of Spain's failing in this regard. Of course, bull fighting is cruel and should be forever consigned to history, but the situation with dogs in Spain is that they are usually working animals used to hunt or protect livestock, and in this respect are no different to many other working animals. This is not dissimilar to how livestock is regarded in Britain, as well as working farm dogs such as Border Collies, and hunt hounds such as Lurchers, Beagles or Welsh Hounds.

Spanish shelters and pounds deal with a never-ending stream of stray and abandoned dogs.

It's always hard for dogs who were once pets to adjust to shelter life.

Tinker Bell with her foster mum, Trina.

Above, right: Charlotte del Rio runs a Galgo sanctuary in southern Spain.

Right: Pauline and Terry currently look after around twenty-five dogs.

A group of dogs at one of our foster homes in Spain.

A rescued Galgo, in a foster home, at the start of his recovery.

I have learned that, in Spain, British expatriates welcome dogs into their homes, treat them as pets, and then ruthlessly dispose of them should they leave to return to the UK, preferring to ship the soft furnishings and television, rather than the animal for whom they have thus far been responsible ... In my opinion, the situation with regard to how the Spanish treat their hounds is partly a case of lack of education, and the commonly-held belief that the dogs are strictly working animals, but calm and rational discussion about the benefits of neutering and microchipping can bring about an understanding and willingness to change. I do find it harder to understand how British people can be responsible for the abandonment of so many dogs, and cannot ignore the fact that this contributes greatly to the stray problem.

I am often asked why it is that we are helping dogs in Spain when we have our own welfare issues in the United Kingdom. My reasons behind this are many and varied, but, primarily, a great many well-funded dog rescue organisations already exist in the UK, and the public is made aware of animal abuse cases via the media and well-financed advertising campaigns. In addition, I hold the view that, as citizens of the world, and a nation of tourists and travellers, an animal in need is the responsibility of humanity as a whole, and not subject to arbitrary boundaries or borders. A suffering dog or cat has no choice

Prince, a starved Galgo rescued from the Spanish pound; now being cared for at Charlotte Del Rio's Galgo sanctuary in southern Spain.

about where he or she may live, and, arguably, is usually in distress because of man. As a comparatively affluent nation, we should be able to help those communities less well off than ourselves, for whom animal welfare is a sometimes unavoidably low priority.

Spain has the largest population of British expatriates in Europe. Our compatriots are happy to live the dream when times are good but, when things turn sour, don't appear to have a problem with discarding their loyal dogs, and turning their backs on a country and lifestyle they had previously embraced.

Forever homes

My parents have a place in Spain, and my mum was planning a short trip to their villa, so we arranged for her to visit Pedro in the shelter to see how he was getting on. Whilst there she called me to sheepishly enquire how to go about adopting a dog and bring him back to England. Our

Their breed indicates that hunters most likely dumped these dogs, who are now in a Galgo sanctuary.

family dog had died many years ago, and my parents had always asserted they would not get another, as they enjoyed the freedom this allowed. Yet, not altogether unsurprisingly, my mum had fallen for a small fluffy dog that had been given up by his previous owners and handed into SOS Animals (of course, I guessed it would be hard for her to go to the shelter and not fall for one of the sad little faces).

So, Freddy flew into Manchester airport, and lives with mum and dad in his forever home in Yorkshire: much-loved and thoroughly spoilt. Acting as a surrogate grandchild, Freddy has reduced the pressure on Sam and I to provide the real thing!

Freddy has recently been joined by Tali, another SOS Animals dog, rescued and taken to the shelter after being found dumped in a plastic bag. Prior to taking Tali, my parents fostered two little terrier-type puppies from SOS Spain, who stayed with them for two weeks before going on to their forever home. Freddy has obviously opened the floodgates ...

Pedro disappears

I decided that I would be able to go to Spain for the last few days of Pedro's time at the shelter, to help out, take some photos for the shelter's website, and have some fun with Pedro and Adrian and really get to know them. Once Pedro's paperwork was complete the plan was that they would both return with me via a ferry from Santander. Iyela and Zora, my rescue dogs from Israel, had had to endure six agonising months of quarantine at Heathrow, and I was looking forward to passing through the airport without the need for this.

However, when I arrived at the shelter I received awful news. While being walked the previous night, Pedro and Adrian had slipped their collars and bolted into the countryside, and had been missing for a day. Though devastated at the news I instantly began to search the local area for the missing pair, realising that getting angry and blaming others would not help find the two boys. I contacted all of the local vets, made posters, and asked everyone I met if they had seen dogs matching their description. I did get quite a few funny looks as I did this, because, of course, there was always an abundance of strays roaming the streets. Equally, though, I received great support and concern from others I came across.

I had arrived in Spain at around three in the afternoon, and covered about ten miles that day, searching the countryside for Pedro and Adrian. Sleeping very little that night, I was out again at dawn to continue.

During my search I was repeatedly told that local hunters had been leaving out poisoned bait and shooting stray dogs, a common occurence during the hunting season to prevent strays interfering with their packs. I learned that many pet dogs had been poisoned as a result of this, which was very negative and upsetting, although small, generous gestures really helped me carry on: a Spanish man I met kept calling to see if I was okay, and offered me a German Shepherd dog of his own; another generous local offered his umbrella. Torrential rain meant that the clothes I had packed were soon filthy, and my only pair of jeans were soaked and ripped: I'd filled my case with dog treats and toys, leads and medication for the shelter, and only enough clothes for the three-night stay I'd planned. A Spanish farmer advised I should hang my underwear on a tree for the dogs to find my scent but I decided against this course of action ...

I'd heard it was common for strays to be taken and tied up as guard dogs and, because of Pedro's and Adrian's size and appearance, was concerned that this could be their fate. Reports and sightings of dogs matching their description constantly raised my hopes, only for them to be dashed each time. Reports of bodies being found filled me with dread until I was able to check them out and confirm that they were not those of the boys. Refusing to give up or let any negative thoughts creep in, I kept telling myself that Pedro and Adrian were still alive and I would find them. I just had to keep on looking.

After eight days of searching – with many advising me to give up – a Dutch family discovered a dog in their garden, frothing at the mouth, bleeding through his nose, convulsing and fitting violently. The kind family managed to get the animal to a local vet, leaving a hundred euros with the instruction that the vet do whatever he could to help him. Adrian had also been seen but they were unable to catch him, and he was gone by the time they returned after taking Pedro to the vet.

I received a call informing me that a dog matching Pedro's description had been taken to a local vet, and I arrived to find Pedro very thin and having difficulty walking. I could barely believe that it was him. He tried to lift his head and wag his tail when he saw me, and although he looked truly awful, it was still the best feeling to finally see my boy.

It seemed as though Pedro's brain was unable to send the right messages to his legs, and the vet was very concerned that there were neurological problems. As already mentioned, it's not uncommon for farmers and hunters to leave out poisonous bait, and it was entirely possible that Pedro had eaten some. Pedro had stopped convulsing, thankfully, but was unable to move, despite receiving fluids and other treatment, appearing almost paralysed in parts of his body. It was very hard to see him like that. The vets told me they would do the best they could for Pedro, and I tried to remain positive with the thought that at least he was now safe and warm.

I now split my time between visiting Pedro and continuing the search for Adrian. The weather was horrendous still, with unseasonal storms filling the dry riverbeds and turning the arid and dusty Spanish campo (countryside) to mud. After remaining positive for so long, I was beginning to seriously worry that there was little hope for Adrian.

A few days later I received news of yet another sighting of a German Shepherd-type dog not far from where Pedro was found. I rushed there to discover that this was a young bitch outside a villa. However, as we turned the car round I noticed what I thought might be a dog lying by a rock, although the lashing rain made it hard to see exactly what it was. As I approached the mass, I could make out what looked like a bag of bones, which grumbled at me as I got closer, but then just flopped and gave up fighting. It was Adrian. He was very scared, and it took the help of a volunteer to gently move him into the car so that I could rush him to the vet. He was very thin and, although conscious, was clearly struggling.

As soon as Pedro and Adrian met at the vet their tails started wagging and both boys seemed to perk up. It was so touching to see, like long-lost friends reuniting. Adrian was put on a drip and we worked on getting him warm. He had fluid in his lungs, and was showing all the signs of severe malnutrition and exposure. Returning the next morning, I spent the entire day with my two boys, trying to get them to eat small meals, and stroking them. I could hardly believe that the three of us were together at last.

The following day I received a phone call around midday, just before my afternoon visit, to say that Adrian had passed away in his sleep. Already physically and mentally drained, I was absolutely distraught at Adrian's death, yet knew I needed to be strong as Pedro was still fighting on.

After two weeks, Pedro was well enough to leave the surgery. His had been an astonishing recovery, and there had been a point early on when the vet had sat me down for a serious discussion about whether or not to put Pedro to sleep. As a last resort I had called my vet in London for advice, and he spoke to the Spanish vet, suggesting that an anti-inflammatory may help reduce the swelling around Pedro's brain. I had been contemplating driving to Madrid to see a specialist in neurology, but left it for a day to see how Pedro responded to the new treatment. First thing the following morning I received a call urgently summoning me to the surgery. Fearing the worst, I rushed there, and could not believe my eyes when I was met by a wobbly – yet standing – Pedro. He had responded really well to the anti-inflammatory drugs and had even eaten: although still frail, he was looking so much better. I was so happy and just hugged his big, soppy head while he stood, supporting himself against my shoulder.

So, I was very excited when the vet finally said that Pedro could be discharged from the clinic as long as I continued to monitor him. The vets were equally amazed at Pedro's recovery, and showed him off to anyone and everyone who came to the clinic. As a rural veterinary practice, they were mostly used to treating hunting dogs, and affectionately referred to him as 'Pedro Increíble' (Pedro the Incredible). When we finally left the clinic, they presented me with a wonderful hamper of dog gifts, including a water bowl, treats, a grooming kit and a dried pig's ear. I think they had fallen for the boy as much as I had!

Convalescence

All of my (extended) stay in Spain I had been living at the house of an amazingly generous volunteer, who was more than happy for Pedro to stay also until he was fully recovered. Kelly and her husband, Phil, already had fifteen rescue dogs, a few cats and a horse at their villa, so Pedro slotted into this menagerie with ease. He would need time to convalesce before he was ready to travel, so I began to give thought to how we could make the journey in the most stress-free way possible.

Pedro required four small meals a day in order to slowly build his strength, and constant monitoring for the first forty-eight hours after leaving the vet, returning there for regular blood tests. Yet back at the villa it was wonderful

Pedro on the road to recovery at Kelly's and Phil's house, weighing around 14kg (30lb).

The memorial fruit tree I planted for Adrian.

to see him begin to play with the other dogs and respond to the routine, affection and security of a home environment, at night sleeping very soundly on the end of my bed. It was such a shame that Adrian could not be part of this with us.

The incredibly tolerant, understanding and patient Sam had been at home alone with Iyela for over a month by this time, as my planned three-day visit to Spain had turned into an epic six-week marathon. We arranged for Sam to fly to Spain and we would rent a car and drive with Pedro back to England via the Channel Tunnel. With many people leaving Spain to return to England, one-way car and van rental firms had sprung up to accommodate the expatriate exodus, and, as there was no way we would ever leave Pedro again (so no flight and no ferry), this was ideal for our needs. Sam's travel arrangements out to Spain entailed first driving from London to Yorkshire to drop off Iyela at my parents,' and a flight the following morning from Leeds Bradford airport. I must remember to thank him again.

Right: Just 4 to 5 weeks later, my boy had filled out and regained his health. Truly, Pedro the Incredible.

I think Sam was somewhat overwhelmed when he arrived at Kelly's and Phil's villa to see me surrounded by fifteen dogs and Pedro. He managed to retain his composure but I know he was a little shocked. Sam grew up with dogs, but to have that many greet you takes some getting used to. Pedro gloriously charged around the garden, showing off and playing.

Going home

The three of us left at six that evening for the drive to England, stopping only one night at a roadside hotel in mid-France, cheerfully paying an extra six euros to enable Pedro to stay in the room with us. He was even allowed to sit by our table as we had dinner that night: only in France are dogs treated so civilly.

Pedro had been on a strict diet of chicken and rice since his ordeal, but I thought it appropriate that he should have his present from the Spanish vets that evening. Back in the room, I gave him the dried pig's ear, which he delightedly threw into the air, circling it as it lay on the bedroom floor and rubbing his body against it. He didn't seem to know exactly what to do with the treat, but it made him happy, nevertheless.

Our journey home to London was easy and speedy in the rented estate car, Pedro stretched out in the back. He was a wonderful traveller and settled down really quickly. After twenty-five hours on the road, we were finally home – and with Pedro!

Chapter three

Spanish hounds

During my unexpectedly extended stay in Spain I had been thinking of how I could help with the overwhelming numbers of dogs at the SOS Animals shelter. I had tentatively dabbled with trying to generate publicity in the United Kingdom, and inform the public about the role the British play in the problem of dumped dogs, but with mixed results.

Additionally, I was continually trying to gather donated vet supplies, bedding, toys, leads, and food to send out to the SOS Shelter in Spain.

While working closely with SOS Animals and Kelly – and really inspired by the work that they were doing – I decided that I could conceivably foster a number of dogs, and try and rehome them in the United Kingdom. I already had a possible home lined up for two dogs at the shelter, and we chose some additional candidates that we felt it would not be too difficult to find homes for.

The Ibizan hounds and Podenco mixes are truly stunning dogs, and, amongst the breeds and types we have in Britain, nothing is similar-looking. Yet, on the Iberian

continued page 52

Jasper waited three years in the shelter until we found him a home in England.

Above: Most shelters are full to capacity – and beyond.

Inset: The Podenco-type dog is the most common found in shelters around Spain.

Main: A resident at the SOS shelter: waiting, hoping ...

Peninsula they are so common that they are not sought-after, and, sadly, are therefore often destined to live out their lives on the streets or in a shelter. Just as the dog shelters in England are currently flooded with Staffordshire Bull Terriers and their like, the Spanish shelters and pounds are inundated with Podenco types.

A dog should never be rehomed on looks alone, of course, but unfortunately, appearance motivates many people. The most important thing is to match the individual needs and character of a dog to a prospective home, which ensures that the match will go as smoothly as possible, and all of a dog's needs wll be met with regard in particular to exercise, energy levels, confidence, sociability, and age. Yet I could not ignore the fact that the Podenco's striking appearance does help to generate an initial enquiry. Podencos are pretty rare in northern Europe, let alone the UK, and, after living in north London, it seems to me that they make perfect Richmond or Hampstead dogs; usually seen strutting on the common or heath with their well-heeled owners. The reality of homing a Podenco is that they need a very secure garden and a good exercise routine, but on looks alone, there's no doubt they are the 'super models' of the dog world.

First UK arrivals

Subsequently, with much planning, a flight from Malaga, and the help of my credit card, Odin, Julieta, Bruiser, Kyle, Micky and Maria arrived on British soil in December 2008.

Podencos, although very hardy, also love their home comforts.

Super models of the canine world: look at those cheekbones!

Bruiser and Julieta waiting in the shelter for their forever homes.

Shelter life can be tough.

We chose to fly them as Micky was not in the best of health, and we wanted the journey to be as quick and easy as possible. Odin and Julieta are Podencos, and both were rehomed by a couple who live by Hampstead Heath (!) in north London, after initial fostering by Sam and me. Odin, a smaller-type Podenco (like a whippet) was an ex-hunting dog reject who was handed over to SOS, and Julieta is a large-type Podenco: the pair make a perfect picture as they prance around on Hampstead Heath. Both dogs are absolutely adored by their owners, Nicky and Greg.

Me with our first UK foster dogs.

A very timid Podenco in the shelter.

Bruiser is a scruffy mixed breed, and Kyle is Julieta's brother: both were rehomed to a couple who live in Surrey. All four dogs were facing life in the shelter (three had been there since they were puppies) and, like so many other dogs in shelters, theirs would have been the sad tale of young, healthy dogs growing old, without ever having had a home of their own.

Finding homes for these two pairs of dogs was the beginning of SOS Animals UK. I am still in contact with both homes, and seeing the four dogs blossom into the characters they are today is very rewarding. Micky and Maria stayed with us and their stories are told later in the book as case studies.

Sam took a little time to get used to having the new foster dogs in the house. The morning after they arrived he awoke very early to the sound of doggy moaning, and went downstairs to investigate. Unfortunately, in his bare feet, he very quickly discovered the cause of the doggy cries ... between his toes ... He cleaned up the mess and, when I awoke a little later, I found him sitting up in a dog bed snoozing, with Maria and Micky wrapped around him.

SOS Animals UK

After lengthy discussion with SOS Spain it was suggested that I run the UK branch of the shelter, concentrating on finding homes for the long-timers, and other dogs it would be difficult to find homes for in Spain, freeing up space and time so that the shelter could continue the great work it was doing. Additionally, I would always see what I could do if made aware of a welfare case, but initially my focus would be the overwhelming population at the Spanish shelter, and the large number of dogs being cared for by fosterers. The shelter already had a similar relationship with volunteers in Sweden, and many of the dogs were being homed in Sweden: the logistics of Europe-wide rehoming was simpler than might be thought ...

After more lengthy correspondence and discussion, we chose eight possible canine candidates to come to England where they would be fostered and ultimately rehomed: it was agonising, trying to pick just eight dogs when so many would be left behind. This time, a flight was out of the question because of the expense, and we had to decide which would be the best way to transport these lucky few.

Sam came to the rescue as he often does. He was

Two long-termers at the shelter.

working at a local comprehensive school, and the October half-term was not far off. I proposed he made a little trip to Spain, flying out to Malaga and picking up a rented van with the dogs already loaded by shelter volunteers, and driving back to the UK. I would stay at home and hold the fort with our dogs and the foster dogs. Surprisingly, he jumped at the offer. Roping in a friend to share the driving, off they went, collecting eight dogs from the shelter: Zack the Mastin Español; Ringo the Pointer mix; Dusty and Diesel (best described as mini wolves); Dexter the Podenco cross German Shepherd; Naomi the Podenco; Rufus the white Shepherd cross, and Paddy the Podenco cross. They completed the round trip in two days and arrived home slightly dazed and confused (Sam and his friend that is: the dogs took it all in their stride). (Some of these early rescues are covered in more detail as case studies.)

From these initial steps into the world of dog rescue matters seemed to gather pace quite rapidly. By the end of the first year (since bringing back Pedro) we had rehomed around fifty dogs in Britain. I set up a website (before this we had been using dog forums and word-of-mouth), and began to develop a network of foster homes throughout the country.

All change

Sam and I had always intended to move out of London to the country, to try and live more self-sufficiently; our dog rescue work was further incentive to leave the city. It was interesting, to say the least, trying to sell our small house in London whilst fostering so many dogs: we had nine, including our own, in residence. We felt that this large canine population may not be very conducive to an early sale, and may, in fact, put off prospective purchasers who viewed our house. Happily, we came up with a solution.

When a viewing was arranged, Sam would take seven of the dogs in the camper van, park around the corner, and sit with them until the viewing was over. He dreaded any of our neighbours seeing him parked up in our very recognisable camper van, as they would usually wander over for a chat, and to ask why he was sitting on the side of the road (probably assuming there'd been some kind of domestic upset). When this happened, the van-full of dogs would leap up, bark, and want to say hello to the friendly visitor at the window, with Sam constantly worried that the noise would give the game away! When it was safe for them to return home I would either call Sam or flash the lights in the window to give him the all-clear. Using this quite laborious technique, eventually, at the beginning of 2011, we managed to sell our house, and purchased a 7 acre smallholding in Powys, Wales.

Unable to immediately occupy our new home, we set about trying to find somewhere to rent for three months on a short lease, but with nine dogs and four cats it was quite a challenge. Sam spent two days on the phone, calling around estate agents to see if anyone could accommodate our unique family. Fortunately, a wonderful estate agent had a place he was developing for himself, just outside Brecon, and was happy to put us up for the three months. The rented property had a two-acre field we could exercise the dogs in, and a large barn where we could house some of the more robust foster dogs. Best of all, it was just a forty minute drive from the house we had bought. Sam had been calling estate agents from Yorkshire to Cornwall and from Norfolk to Snowdonia, and to find a place so close to our new home was extremely lucky. We'd visions of having to live on a camp site for three months! Only in Wales could this have been achieved, as the Welsh seemed far less perturbed by our unique setup than did most people.

After three months of renting the house near Brecon we moved into our own property in Radnorshire, Powys. The previous owners had had twelve cats living on their land that they said were feral, and were intending to take them to the coast to release them to fend for themselves, as they were moving to France and would not take the cats with them. We were, understandably, not very happy with the idea of twelve cats, used to being fed every day, fending for themselves through a Welsh winter. Several of them were quite elderly and had various medical conditions.

As a result of this, on arrival at our new house we inherited a small band of felines to add to our already extended furry family, and they are the most affectionate and tame 'feral' cats I have ever known, who turn up at the same time every day to be fed. I have contemplated trying to find homes for some of these felines, but they are so used to their semi-feral life that it would be a struggle for them to adapt to a more domestic routine. On the odd occasion when I have had to take any to the vet, they panic in the cat carry crate, and find the whole ordeal very traumatic.

At our new house we built a small, heated kennels, although generally the dogs are fostered in the house, and I had, by this time, developed a large group of foster homes in Spain and throughout the UK. A foster home really helps acclimatise a dog to what life in Britain will be like: getting used to strange, new experiences such as television, telephones, house guests, car journeys, and family life makes the ultimate transition to their new home as stress-free as possible. A fosterer gets to know a dog's character really well, and can provide invaluable information when it comes to making decisions about the right home for him or her.

'Failed' fostering

One possible and lovely outcome of fostering is what I call a 'failed' fosterer: someone who decides that they can't possibly hand over their charge after all, and who takes on the dog permanently. Of course, then, unfortunately, I've lost a foster home, unless they are willing to continue fostering, but that is nothing compared with the fact that a dog has found a forever home (I have to admit that Sam and I have been failed fosterers a couple of times ...).

Unfortunately, a downside of our move to Wales was that Sam sold the camper van. The Bus' lowered suspension did not take kindly to the rutted track and lack of tarmac that is the road to our house (through three farm gates). Sam did attempt it a couple of times, but more out of bravado than any real expectation of success. Our replacement vehicle is a warm, reliable, practical – and soulless – four-wheeled-drive truck. It is lovely to drive, the heating works, and it starts every time, yet, occasionally, I catch Sam looking on Volkswagen enthusiast websites, and he talks about getting a sixteen inch VW Type 25 syncro, whatever that is.

Work with the dogs had progressed apace since the early days in London, and in January 2013 alone we rehomed 15 dogs. My daily routine consists of walking, feeding (administering medication hidden in scraps of chicken); cleaning, canine diplomatic liaison, replying to email and phone enquiries, European doggy logistics, chats with fosterers, and website updates. We have no

'Failed' fostering.

employed staff, only a core of very dedicated volunteers and foster homes, and a larger group of generous supporters, who have helped us find around four hundred dogs their forever homes. We also send volunteers, veterinary students and vets to the shelter in Spain to help out, and support neutering programmes.

Part of the work I now do means being surrounded by a large number of dogs, pretty much all of the time. Unless you've experienced this, it's hard to properly appreciate the joy, agony, frustration and humour that make up managing pack life, which is totally different to life with just a couple of dogs. At our home, Sam and I have our own dogs, long-term foster dogs (medical issues, very timid, old age and therefore most likely to be with us for the rest of their lives), and short-term foster dogs looking for homes.

Having a pack of dogs requires quite careful management at times, especially when a new foster dog needs to be introduced. We know the characters, individual doggy political views, and potential grumpiness of certain pack members, and once a new arrival has been accepted (with our guidance) by the upper echelons of the pack, it is not long before they are sleeping together, eating together, and charging around the garden barking and causing trouble together. We concentrate on keeping our dogs safe, secure, happy and exercised. We walk dogs in small groups and have securely fenced off a run in our woodland, with a double-gate 'air-lock' entrance, so they can get up to speed in a large area off-lead (any Podenco will need to run, prance and jump). A few pack members can sit and stay, and a couple will very politely offer you a paw, but we do not have the time to dedicate to on-going training, and, in any case, this will be done in their forever home.

continued page 60

Goodbye London; hello Wales!

The pack enjoying the view in Brecon, Wales.

Spike and Fox enjoying our woodland.

The pack manages itself very well under our leadership: yes, there are instances of orchestral howling on the rare occasion when we both leave the house, but this stops after two minutes to be replaced by a game of sleeping lions. All of our guests are, necessarily, dog lovers, and, when they visit, we tell them the best thing to do is enter confidently, ignore the dogs, sit down, and the pack will chill out – eventually. There are moments when you want to pull your hair out in frustration, equally matched by moments of utter joy, and there is nothing quite like curling up on the sofa with a pack of hounds, basking in the unconditional love they give. It puts a pair of chewed trainers into perspective.

Progress

On a recent trip to Spain I saw how SOS Animals Spain has changed since I first turned up with Pedro. Moving to a new location, the number of dogs in its care has decreased, as it was decided it would be better to concentrate on a few dogs at a time to ensure that they could be properly assessed, cared for, and rehomed as effectively as possible. This also means that those animals in long-term care get the best quality of life. Although the stray situation in Spain has not really changed, and the countryside is still full of homeless canines, the work that the shelter does is now far more manageable and less overwhelming. As I write this, SOS Spain has around 60 dogs in its care at the shelter, and a further number in foster homes.

I could never have imagined how things would turn out when I decided to take on those first foster dogs; certainly, I had no intention of establishing a UK branch of SOS Animals, or expectation of it developing into what it has become. I just knew that I wanted to help those dogs in need as I could not ignore the problem.

What gives me great hope is that we now seem to be working more with Spanish locals and younger generations, too. The tide does seem to be slowly turning, and we now

continued page 66

Overleaf:
Left: A tender moment.

Right: I just love Pedro's big, soppy face.

Foster dog meets hoover bag ...

A volunteer at SOS Animals Spain.

Our pack.

have English, Swedish and Spanish volunteers helping us rescue stray dogs. This is a big shift from how it was and is very encouraging. Although there are still huge numbers of stray dogs and pounds full of unwanted animals, the public in Spain seems more aware of the broader issues regarding animal welfare, and the role that hunters and expatriates play in creating the problem.

Simply finding homes for those dogs currently without one will not resolve the larger issues: the strays are, after all, a symptom, not the cause. Shelters and rescue centres are full to bursting, and healthy dogs – including puppies and pedigree animals – are euthanized on a weekly basis. In the past, dogs were bred to undertake a certain role or job such as hunting, guarding, swimming or herding, but nowadays are rarely required to participate in these activities. Changing fashions and trends can dictate the requirement for a specific look, breed, type or size of dog, and the majority of dogs are chosen for their appearance and – often misconceived – idea of temperament. It's a very sad fact that, when considering getting a dog, many prospective owners will not even contemplate a rescue dog for a variety of reasons. They may have in mind a specific breed, completely unaware that most have a dedicated rescue organisation: from a chocolate Labrador to a West Highland White Terrier, all can be found in shelters and rescue centres throughout the world. It's a commonly-held misconception that rescue dogs will have behavioural problems, and that getting a pedigree dog will ensure a certain character-type and temperament. But generally rescue centres – and certainly ours – will go to great lengths to match dogs with owners, at the same time ensuring that the animal's specific needs will be met in their new home.

Finding homes for strays and dogs in shelters is sometimes akin to chipping away at an immense glacier which grows quicker than it's possible to deplete. I am inundated with requests for help from caring individuals who have found dogs in need, and constantly being made aware of animal abuse and welfare cases. My email inbox is often full, generally with heartbreaking photos attached, and the phone rings seven days a week. The more dogs I find homes for the greater my network of like-minded people and incidence of animals in need, and having to decide who stays and who goes; who to help and who I can't is agonising. All of the good people I have met and continue to meet, who enable me to carry on through their generosity and effort, give me so much encouragement and support. Being a small rescue concern means I can really take care and match a dog with a home: not a quick process, which can be difficult at times when many homes are not suitable for a particular dog. But the end result of knowing that a dog has found his or her forever home always confirms to me that we are on the right track. By concentrating on a few dogs at a time we have managed to struggle on without becoming too stressed, and I have, to date, managed to keep my sanity – just!

To banish forever the problem of unwanted animals, there needs to be a huge shift in attitude and culture, and better education for all, but especially our children. We simply must stop breeding more dogs for a certain look or temperament, which is morally wrong when shelters and rescue centres are full of healthy dogs that are put to sleep for lack of a home. I will never understand how someone can buy a puppy when somewhere there is a puppy of the same breed languishing in a shelter, or being put to death. From the hunter who hangs his old hunting dog when the season is over to the Pug and Chihuahua 'handbag dogs' that now fill Californian shelters, we must educate and inform people of the misery that their actions can cause. Neutering incentives and mandatory microchipping are positive ways of addressing the stray population, but on their own are not a solution: the depressing reality is that most acts of animal charity treat only the symptoms without ever finding a cure.

Every time thoughts such as these threaten to weigh me down, all I need do is look at one of the many photos of the dogs we have rescued, luxuriating on the sofa in their new home; glance at the contented foster dogs sleeping around me, or look at Pedro's big, soppy face. Every dog, no matter where he or she is from, or what they look like, is worthwhile, and rewards me over and over again. The stress of rescuing and rehabilitating a dog – the fostering, transporting, finding a home for and constantly worrying about the animal – is always repaid with smiles and lovely photos of sleeping, happy dogs. I do not do this work for reward or thanks, and am well aware that I will never resolve the problem on my own. But that does not mean I should do nothing. The motto of SOS Animals UK says it all, really: "Changing one dog's life at a time."

Chapter four

Give a dog a home

Every dog we rescue is a case study. They all have their own stories and unique histories, and, of course, new, hopeful futures now. To pick out just a few is hard, but there are some that stick in our minds for whatever reasons, be it personal connection, individual character, or the shocking circumstances. What follows are a selection of case studies that I hope show the transition from street to sofa. They all have very happy endings.

Georgia, the Podenco Maneto

Georgia was found wandering on the side of a motorway near Cádiz. She was incredibly thin, with a skeletal appearance, and near to death. By the look of her excessively saggy undercarriage she had clearly recently given birth to a litter, and had possibly been dumped because she was then surplus to requirements.

As mentioned earlier, Podenco Manetos are used to hunt small prey such as rabbits, as they are so good at getting into thick undergrowth and flushing out quarry. They are a classic rural hunting dog in Spain, so almost certainly a hunter had abandoned her. Georgia is probably about seven or eight years old, so would have been considered at the end of her usefulness. She had most likely been wandering the countryside for a long time, judging by her emaciated condition when she was found.

We were asked to help and placed Georgia in a foster home in Antequera, where she spent six months and, although quite timid, was gradually returned to full health. It was discovered that Georgia had heartworm, which required three months of intensive treatment. Heartworm is a serious condition and the treatment can be quite aggressive, but Georgia is a tough little girl and she pulled through. She bonded with a little Miniature Pinscher called Rosy who was clearly helping Georgia adapt to life as a domestic pet. Georgia was very wary of people, and had obviously been treated quite roughly by her previous owner. Even now, she still tends to freeze or cower if you move too quickly. Despite this, she loves affection, and is never happier than when she is rolling on her back in a comfy bed.

Georgia and Rosy came to the UK to be fostered by us in December 2011. Sam fell for her instantly and he can be blamed for the fact that she is now one of our dogs. Georgia's bond with Rosy is very strong, and clearly gives her confidence, so for the time being they are both staying with us. A classic case of failed fostering, I think ...

Despite Georgia's squat frame and short legs there is serious hunting pedigree in her, and she charges about on our land, oblivious to the change in climate, yelping and sticking her nose into the dense undergrowth in vain attempts to hunt. She never catches anything, but this

Georgia: a tough little girl ...

... who also enjoys her home comforts.

little dynamo dashes about, powered by instinct, hunting phantom rabbits. It's a real pleasure to see her satisfied and happy, both in and out of the house. She can still be a little wary and skittish, but every day she grows in confidence. Sam has a real soft spot for her, and likes to think that she worships him (I think she does, a little).

I can't talk about Georgia and Rosy without mentioning the wonderful people who fostered and cared for the two of them in Spain. Pauline and Terry originally moved from near The Black Mountains in Wales to Antequera in Spain to retire and breed dogs, but soon realised the situation in Spain was so awful that breeding dogs was morally inappropriate. Since then the couple have dedicated all of their time – and their home – to fostering and helping dogs in need. They have bid goodbye to conventional furniture, as the dogs destroyed anything soft, and instead sit on deck chairs that they pull out each night to watch the television. Their entire garden has been tiled

to make it easy to power-hose clean, and is surrounded by a mesh fence. At one point they were caring for over sixty dogs, and have never turned away a single dog. These are the quiet heroes of the world: asking for no support or funding, just acting as their consciences dictate.

On an ongoing basis we try and help Pauline and Terry find homes for their dogs, and working with them is always a life-affirming experience. They are yet another example of the wonderful people I have met through rescuing dogs who ask not for praise or thanks for the work they do, but only support.

Tula, the Chihuahua cross, and Foxy, the Corgi cross

Via the network of SOS volunteers and fosterers I was informed that two dogs had been left in Calais at the border vets. When travelling with dogs using the UK pet passport scheme, the animals are required to have a veterinary check-up between 48 and 24 hours before travelling. The two dogs – which SOS Animals had helped with – had been abandoned by their British owners (who had taken the ferry to England regardless) as one of the dog's passports had not been correctly filled out when issued. The usual outcome in a case such as this is that French Customs would have kept them for a period of time before having them put to sleep.

Once again, through the networks I had established, I managed to find someone who was travelling back to the United Kingdom, and arranged for Tula and Foxy to be picked up by these generous people, and we would meet them on their return to England. I had to get one of my friends who spoke French to explain the position to the vet and make sure they held on to the pair for me. The two dogs had been at the French vet for five days by the time they were collected, and both were very scared.

Tula was about nine years old and Foxy was about 14. We knew who had done the passports for them, so were able to glean some of their history. Tula was initially rescued from a shelter as a puppy, while Foxy had been found on the streets in Fuengirola on the Costa del Sol when she was about three. They had not been mistreated – a little over-fed maybe – and had clearly been loved pets. Their original owners did eventually get in touch, but said they were in rented accommodation and not in a position to have them as both were in poor health. Forced to leave Spain for financial reasons that they said were a result of the

Tula and Foxy – inseparable friends.

economic downturn, they simply could not cope with what had happened.

Tula and Foxy were devoted to each other so would have to be rehomed together. Finding a home for two dogs is not an easy task, and especially two dogs of a more mature age, but these two simply could not be separated. They very obviously gave each other huge support, grooming each other so very gently and curling up in a ball together.

Health-wise, Foxy had a few lumps on her, and her teeth were in a very poor state. We had all her lumps checked out to see if any were cancerous, and she had about five teeth removed. Fortunately, none of her lumps were problematic, and once she had her bad teeth out she was like a puppy again (they must have been very uncomfortable for her). We also discovered that Tula had a very bad heart murmur that would need ongoing treatment.

When the pair first arrived they were both very confused, and Foxy was a bit grumpy and growly (it took us a while to realise that Foxy would grumble and growl when she was happy, excited, angry, playful, sleepy and hungry: she used one word for everything to great effect). Happily, it was not long before the two of them were contentedly curled up on our bed.

After more than a year of fostering these two little ladies, with no success in finding them a home, we decided that they would be long-term foster dogs with us. By now, Foxy was about 15 and Tula about ten, and we felt it would not be right for them to be moved on at their advanced ages.

Foxy is a tyical Corgi: wilful, stubborn, and food-obsessed. We love her even more for her character foibles and she frequently makes us laugh out loud. Tula is a little madam, and is the top dog in our pack. She rules with an iron paw and keeps everyone in check; she's a real matriarch. The pair follow me around all day as if they have always been with us, and I cannot imagine life without them. Truly small dogs with big characters – and curled up together in a bed at my feet as I type this – we are only too happy to give these girls the retirement they deserve.

Tula: Despite having a heart murmur, Tula showed little sign of the condition, and would run about like a puppy, she had so much energy. It was a joy to watch her running in the fields with Foxy and her best friend, Spike, who she would chase and play with all day long.

However, shortly after writing her case study, Tula began to show symptoms of her condition. She fought on for several months against all the odds – chasing Spike; barking; running about the garden: her will to live simply amazed us. We wanted to make sure that her quality of life was second to none, as we had noticed that her health was deteriorating. Sadly, Tula passed away in my arms on Friday 31 May 2013.

Tula was such a special girl, and although we did not have her very long it felt like she had always been in our lives and belonged with us. She followed us everywhere – our shadow – never leaving our sides, and if we went out her big eyes were always watching for our return.

A little madam with a big heart and character to match, Tula slept in our bed, and very quickly became top dog in our pack. Missed by all of us – but especially by Foxy,

who seems incomplete without her life-long friend – we are so grateful for the privilege of having known Tula, and feel that perhaps it was meant to be that she came to us for the reasons she did, and at the time of her life that she did.

She will always be a massive part of our lives: words cannot express how much she meant to us and how much she will be missed.

Micky, the Podenco

Kelly, who saved me when I was trying to find Pedro, found Micky by some dustbins in a very poor state: a bag of bones and very close to death. She gathered him up and put him in her car, intending to take him to the vet to be put to sleep, but, as she did so, Micky "gave me a smile" as she opened the car. This little sign of fighting spirit persuaded Kelly to give him a chance to see if he could pull through.

Micky tested positive for leishmaniasis, a disease common in the Mediterranean. Caused by the bite of the sandfly, the parasite attacks the immune system, leaving the dog unable to fight infection and disease as well as a healthy animal would. At the moment there is no cure for canine leishmaniasis as the parasite continues to live in the bone marrow, but there are drugs available to manage the disease. If diagnosed and treated early, an infected dog can lead a long and happy life. Special collars are available that offer some protection from the sandfly bite, but obviously strays do not have these and so are frequently exposed.

Micky went home to live with Kelly at her villa. She already had many dogs in her care, but gave Micky all she could to help him in his struggle to recover. He had developed severe arthritis as a result of the leishmaniasis going untreated for such a long time, and, although he was very underweight, his light frame enabled him to be as mobile as he possibly could. Despite all his ailments Micky began to experience what life could be like, and revelled in being a pack member in a loving home. He would trundle around the villa, respected by all the other dogs, as if they knew what he had been through. He was also a bit of a flirt and loved any attention he received from the female dogs, though, sadly for him, could never move quickly enough to take advantage of this!

Another endearing characteristic was Micky's love of cats, and he could often be found very gently playing with them in his bed or on the sofa. I first met Micky when I was at Kelly's villa during the search for Pedro, when he would

Micky with Kelly when she found him.

follow me everywhere, and slept on my bed at night. To say that I fell for this dashing, courteous gent would be an understatement.

To give Micky the best quality of life he could possibly have we decided to bring him to England and adopt him. We were well aware that the little lad would not have too long, and our aim was to make what time he had the best it could possibly be. So Micky came to London in the winter of 2008, and promptly set about breaking the hearts of everyone he met. He was a firm favourite at our allotment, and would follow us around our local woodland, attracting so much attention that our walks would take twice as long. If ever a dog had presence, Micky did.

When his time to leave us finally came it was quick

Micky, Pedro and Maria ready for bed at Kelly's.

Micky and Minty the kitten.

and he made the trip with my husband when Sam drove over during the October holiday in 2008.

Dexter's mouth always appeared to be half open, which was probably a result of being hit in the face at some point. Sam named him Chop Chop on the journey home in 2008, partly because of Dexter's hanging jaw, and partly due to the fact that he could be a bit grumpy at times, but only when he was afraid.

So, after four long years in the shelter Dexter was finally in a foster home and getting used to what life as a dog should really be like. Dexter found his forever home with Ant and Sarah – volunteer dog walkers in London – who, after enquiring about a dog, fell for Dexter's charms while walking him. Sarah and Ant are a yoga teacher and ski instructor respectively, and so Dexter divides his time between Britain and Switzerland, happily travelling on his pet passport, and worshipped by his wonderful owners.

Naomie had been sharing a kennel with Dexter in Spain, and they really helped each other through the tough times of being shelter dogs. Before being rescued, Naomie was known to the volunteers at SOS Animals as she was a stray wandering in the local village. When they finally managed to catch her and get her to the shelter, it was clear that she had been quite badly abused. She was covered in old wounds, scratches and current injuries, and was missing a few teeth. She had been used like a punch bag; kicked and hit on numerous occasions. Despite what she had been through, however, Naomi was incredibly loving and affectionate, and still – amazingly –trusted people.

Like Dexter, Naomie was destined to spend her life at the shelter. There was little possibility of finding her a home in Spain so, again like Dexter, we decided to give her a chance and get her into a foster home in the UK. Naomi travelled with Dexter and spent the entire journey sitting securely between Sam and his friend in the front of the van. Sam really fell for her, and she was, apparently, a great traveller, sitting up at the front of the van like she was helping with the driving, pawing the passenger if he stopped stroking her.

Once in England it was not long before Naomie found her forever home. A family from St Albans, just north of London, had been enquiring about another dog, and, after I suggested Naomie, they seemed keen so we arranged a visit. When they met her we all thought she would be perfect for their situation: a busy household, with children

with little suffering. Micky had twelve great months with us and experienced life as it should be. Had we not taken him in, he would not have lived as long: I feel privileged to have known him and am so grateful we were able to give him the best time of his life.

Dexter, the Podenco cross Shepherd, and Naomie, the Podenco

When I originally became involved with SOS Animals Spain, quite a few of the dogs at the shelter had been there for a number of years, and were most likely destined to spend their entire lives there. Dexter was just a puppy when he arrived at the shelter in Spain, and became one of these long-timers. He had been in the shelter for four years when we decided to take him to be fostered at a home in England,

Dexter and Naomie helped each other in the shelter.
(Courtesy Elin Cidh)

Dexter doing yoga with his mum.
(Courtesy Anthony Cullen)

and foster children. After all that Naomie has been through, she still trusts people, and in truth is quite demanding of love and attention. That is just how some dogs are, giving unconditional love despite their past traumas, and really living in the moment. Naomie is adored by her new owners and revels in all the love she gets from their extended family.

Gemma, the Podenco Ibicenco

In the spring of 2012, I was made aware of a compound where hundreds of dogs were being kept in very grim conditions. It appeared that hunters had been dumping their dogs in this compound, and the animals had been

74

Horrific living conditions inside the compound.
(Courtesy Beverley Farmer)

Above, inset: The camp was full of almost every type of Podenco and Galgo. *(Courtesy Beverley Farmer)*

Left: Mass graves. *(Courtesy Beverley Farmer)*

Two Podencos chained to trees, with little shelter from the elements. *(Courtesy Beverley Farmer)*

left to breed uncontrollably while being provided with a minimum standard of care. The site was full of mass graves with huge piles of semi-buried remains dotted about the place.

In what can only be described as a canine concentration camp, some dogs were chained with little protection from the elements, whilst others roamed free, scratching out a little depression in the hard earth in which to curl up and sleep. The camp was full with almost every type of Podenco and Galgo of every age, from very young puppies to heavily-pregnant bitches. The site was littered with faeces, and was very exposed, with just a few trees for shade.

Access was gained with the help of local authorities, the Spanish police, and various local rescue centres who had come together via Facebook and other networks to try and save as many of the dogs as possible. Sadly, although several of the animals had to be put to sleep as they were beyond help, a larger number were rescued, and Gemma was one of these lucky few.

Although already full, SOS Animals Spain agreed to take on four or five dogs, for whom I was charged with helping to find homes. As is always the case, we ended up taking eight dogs – Mary, Tina, Molly, Ella, Jenny, Gemma, Star and Terri – with the help of another rescue centre. We managed to find Mary a home locally in Spain with an English woman, which was quite a rare achievement. Tina was found a home in Holland, and Jenny, Star and Terri found homes in England. Molly and Ella were rehomed together, also in the UK.

Gemma was about a year old when she was rescued, so most likely had been born at the compound. She spent four months at the shelter where it was discovered that she had tick fever and anaplasmosis, a disease caused by a rickettsial parasite of ruminants. Both conditions were

Left: Gemma in our woods doing what Podencos do best ...

Right: ... and in hunt mode: ears pricked and alert.

treated in the shelter prior to her coming to the UK to be fostered by us in Wales.

Once again, despite her horrific start in life, Gemma is an affectionate and loyal girl who loves dogs and people. It always amazes me how some dogs can experience such brutality, yet emerge psychologically well balanced. She is still a sensitive girl, but with a bomb-proof disposition. Whilst in foster care with us Gemma has fallen for Donelly, another of our foster dogs, a feeling which appears mutual as they are devoted to each other, and constantly play and run about together as if born to it. At the time of writing Gemma and Donelly are still hoping to find permanent homes, although it will be very hard to separate them. We would love to find them a home together, but, as they are both quite big dogs, it's unlikely that this will happen. For the time being they give each other love and support as each waits for their forever home ...

Maria: a very special mix of various things, with some sort of squat-legged Podenco

During my search for Pedro I came across a small dog living in a broken-down van. The van had no engine, and the little dog had been getting in under the bonnet and through the missing dashboard. Her side was covered in sores and open wounds, as if she had been burnt, and she was heavily pregnant. When I tried to coax her out of the van she leapt into my arms and frantically licked me.

I took her back to Kelly's and Phil's villa, and we began treatment of her wounds. The large scar on her side looked like a splash mark, as if caused by corrosive or boiling liquid, and she was missing all the fur along her flank. I named her Maria. Because all of the rescue shelters were (and are) inundated, the decision was taken to abort Maria's puppies. A dreadful thing to have to do but the most responsible action, given the existing problem.

I cannot help trying to piece together a dog's history from whatever physical marks they bear, and their characters and temperaments. It's an unavoidable grimness that comes with animal rescue work, and this dark detective work has also infected my husband after years of living in close vicinity to me. Sam has it that Maria's scar is a result of her scavenging near a kitchen and getting a full pan of something very hot thrown at her by an angry chef. The way that she generally cowered from and barked at men was a

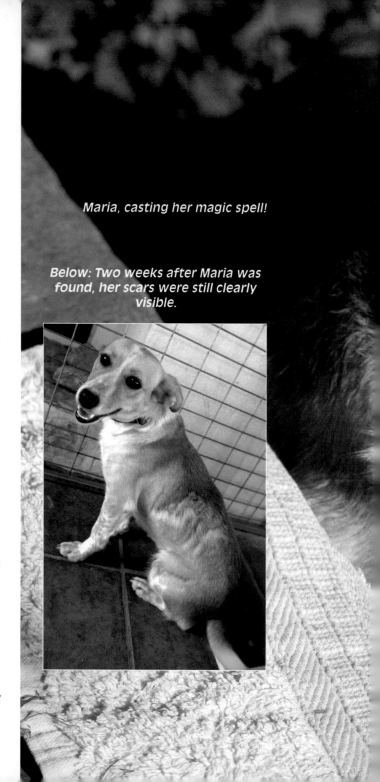

Maria, casting her magic spell!

Below: Two weeks after Maria was found, her scars were still clearly visible.

Iyela and Maria: bridesmaids at our wedding.
(Courtesy Rebecca Roundhill)

at fostering her in London, and Maria had had a chance to wrap him round her little finger. In no time at all she had also completely seduced Pedro, who lets her walk all over him!

Maria is short and squat like a Podenco Maneto, but with a rough, spotty coat, and just high enough off the ground not be held back in a full sprint. She's a little ball of muscle, and is never happier than when she is charging through dense undergrowth or digging out imaginary rabbits. With real Podenco character in a small dog, she could sleep all day or run until she drops, and is an unsurpassed escapologist. There is no garden, field or fence that is Maria-proof. Despite her escapades, however, she is the most loving and affectionate little girl (when not caked in mud).

Maria was a bridesmaid with Iyela at our wedding, and sat next to Pedro, who wore a bandana that informed all-and-sundry of his best man status that day.

Dusty and Diesel, the Husky/Shepherd cross mini wolves, with maybe a little Podenco thrown in

It's impossible to say for certain precisely what breed or pedigree Dusty and Diesel are, as you can tell from my attempt at a title! This is so often the case with rescues and strays who have been left to breed unchecked. The shaggy siblings had been living in an apartment all their lives with only a small, fenced-in balcony as outdoor space. As two extremely high-energy dogs who need exercise and direction to be satisfied, it was incredibly cruel to confine them to a balcony. Like coiled springs ready to explode, there was surely some kind of working hound in their genetics.

Their owner handed the two into the shelter, and I arranged for them to be driven home with Sam. They were both so deeply unhappy at the shelter, and always desperate to be let out of their pen. Some dogs deal with shelter life better than others, but Dusty and Diesel hated being caged or restricted: understandable, after being shut up for so long in the apartment. Sam said that whenever he walked the pair during the journey back to the UK, the

sign that something horrible had happened to her, but, with Phil being both male and well-built, Maria would have to get over this phobia. All credit to Phil because, with patience and a gentle approach, Maria was soon taking her first steps to true recovery just by being around him. She really helped me when I was searching for Pedro, and would leap on my lap when I returned each day, cheering me up. I needed her as much as she needed me.

When Sam flew to Spain to collect me and Pedro, Maria was still at Kelly's house, and she ran round him in circles, barking and growling: it seemed that one man at a time was all she could cope with. No doubt you'll be happy to learn that they now adore each other. I knew that I had fallen for Maria, and would have to start dropping hints and suggestions. Sam eventually came round after we 'failed'

Main: Dusty and Diesel in the shelter at SOS Spain ...

Left: ... and so happy to be out of it!

crate they shared would vibrate with excitement when he approached to put on their leads, and he had to be very careful that they did not make a bolt for freedom when he opened the door.

We fostered the two of them in London, and Diesel quickly latched onto Sam. Both Dusty and Diesel are highly intelligent dogs who need jobs to do if they are to be content. They were close, but not inseparable, and could be rehomed separately with little fuss. In truth, I think they wound each other up slightly, as whenever Dusty ran about Diesel would leap around her and chase her until she stopped.

Luckily, it was not long before a prospective home came along for Dusty, which turned out to be perfect for her. She now lives in Oxfordshire where she is very happy, paired up with the family Whippet. (This lovely couple have recently also taken another dog from us.)

Diesel was still looking for his forever home when we moved to Wales. He is a stunning-looking dog, and photos could never do him justice, making him look bigger than he actually is. Sam loved Diesel and would take him wild camping on the Brecon Beacons.

We had fostered him for nearly a year when a couple looking for their first dog enquired about him. We were slightly concerned about this as we felt that Diesel may need an owner with some experience, but, after meeting them, and them meeting Diesel, we felt more confident that they might make a good match. On a second visit the couple took Diesel to the local pub for lunch, which went well, and so Diesel was collected on a subsequent visit. That Diesel's new owners had driven from the south east of England to Wales on three occasions showed real commitment.

In his new home Diesel has flourished as an only dog, as he really wants all the attention. He is a real 'one man and his dog' type which is why (although this may dent Sam's ego) he latched onto him so resolutely. Strange though it may sound, Diesel really was not a pack dog, and was always far more interested in being involved in people-stuff. Diesel's owners are now married, and receiving videos and pictures of him on patrol in his garden, or curled up on the sofa, is so heart-warming.

Oliver, the Spanish Mastiff cross

On rare occasions I come across cases that I can only

Above: Oliver, when he was rescued from Parque Animal. (Courtesy Rebecca Sierra)

Right: Stanley and Oliver: best of friends.

describe as pure evil, and Oliver's is one such case, although, thankfully, he is now happy and safe.

In 2010 it was discovered that the owners of the Parque Animal, a sanctuary in Torremolinos on the Costa del Sol, had been illegally euthanising cats and dogs in their care. During investigations by the guardia civil (Spanish regional police), evidence was found that the two owners had wrongly been carrying out "massive euthanising" programmes for over a year, by – it was claimed by the prosecution – administering lethal medication in small doses that would cause "unnecessary and unjustified suffering until death." The inhumane pair have subsequently been charged with animal cruelty, and are awaiting trial for illegally killing up to three thousand – yes, three *thousand* – cats and dogs.

SOS Animals Spain was one of a few shelters that became involved in trying to resolve the mess left by Parque Animal. Many of the dogs were in such poor condition that they had to be put to sleep, but Oliver was taken on by Kelly from SOS Animals Spain, and placed in foster care with her. An emergency trip to the vet had seen his tail amputated as

it was severely lacerated and developing necrosis as a result of going untreated. SOS Animals Spain took on a further 14 dogs from Parque Animal.

We found Oliver his forever home through our website. I had been in correspondence with a wonderful prospective home, trying to match them with a dog, and Oliver fitted the bill perfectly. His dedicated new owners already had Stanley, a Labrador, and, after taking on Oliver, decided they also had room for another SOS Animal dog, so their pack increased to three.

The Spanish Mastiff, or Mastín Español, is an awesome dog, and Oliver has some typical Spanish Mastiff characteristics: he is easy-going, gentle and loving, although initially a little wary of strangers. Being a cross breed, Oliver is slighter than average, but these giants can weigh anything from 70 to 120 kilos (150-260 pounds). Originally bred to guard livestock, they have the classic temperament of the loyal flock dog: dignified; calm; intelligent, and devoted to their pack or family. They are often still used in Spain as working dogs, and we have found homes for a number of these soppy mammoths.

Tarzan, the Podenco Campanero, and The Three Musketeers

Tarzan was stuck in the Badajoz perrera (pound), and this gentle lad was a matted and mucky heap of fur. A Podenco Campanero should have a lovely, shaggy white coat, and Tarzan looked so sad with his big, matted dreadlocks and sore eyes.

Some Spanish locals were running a Facebook page that detailed all of the dogs in the perrera, complete with photos, which I could not help but look through. Time was limited for all of the dogs on the appeal as they were soon to be euthanized.

Another photo showed one pen in which three terrified dogs huddled together in a small defensive unit. They were unlike any breed of dog I had ever seen; a combination of Dachshund, Bassett Hound, Corgi and a drop of Mastiff. Three squat and wobbly little lads, with varying degrees of bowed, Queen Anne chair-style legs, stood together with fear in their eyes.

I decided that I could take Tarzan and these three boys, and get them to Pauline and Terry' to be fostered, in addition to which we also saved a further two dogs from the Badajoz perrera. Billie and Eva were also in an horrific state

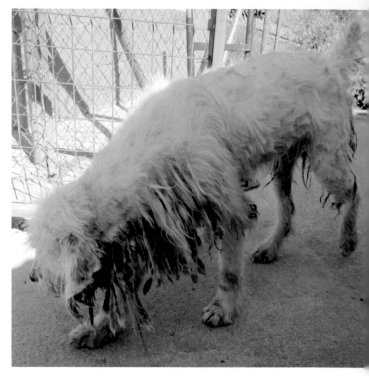

Tarzan, with heavy matted dreadlocks, when he was rescued from the pound ...
(Courtesy Therese Rantzow)

and were sharing a pen with Tarzan. Both, now, are in lovely homes.

One of our supporters, who had helped secure the release of the dogs, named the three boys Porthos, Athos and Aramis, which we thought were great choices. Tarzan was a real gent and took no time at all to get used to foster life, revelling in his new environment, after he had been completely clipped and his ears deep-cleaned and flushed. The boy also had problems with severe eye infections, which require ongoing treatment. The Three Musketeers looked like they could be siblings, or maybe a dad and his two sons, as they were variations of each other. However, they were all very scared, and took a long time to get used to human contact and the foster home environment. With Pauline's and Terry's careful and sensitive help, their confidence slowly

... and looking amazing in his new life. (Courtesy Jenny Spence)

built to the point where they could walk into the house and be around people without bolting outside.

We found Tarzan a home with a family that had previously adopted a Spanish Mastiff from us, and he went straight from the foster home in Spain to his new home in Scotland. We felt that Porthos, Athos and Aramis needed some more work so all three came to us in Wales to be fostered and further rehabilitated.

Over time their confidence grew from the early days when they would urinate and freeze when put on a lead, to finally happily running and playing with us in the garden. A couple of volunteers from SOS Sweden stayed with us for a week, and spent the entire time working with the three lads, getting them used to lead walking.

Athos found his home first and now lives with a mature Collie and a Corgi as his new family. He has his own page on Facebook, and keeps us updated about all the goings-on in his new life. We've been told that he loves barking, and hates training. Porthos went as an only boy to a lovely couple who live in Durham. Out of the three, Porthos

The three boys being fostered in Wales. Note Porthos taking some time out at the back.

was always the most independent, and would sometimes take himself off to bed for some me-time while the others played. Now, as an only dog, we can see how happy he is being doted on and worshipped for the lovely chap he is.

For some reason Aramis was with us for some time before his forever home arrived, when we initially thought he would be the first to go as he was the bravest of the three. A lovely family, who live by Richmond Common in London, has now adopted him. They already own a Pointer cross called Ginger who has accepted Aramis into her family, and it's as if he has always been with them. We are happily amazed at how well Aramis has adapted from the early days when he first arrived.

Betsy, Huéznar, Genil, Bembézar, Viar and Guadiamar, the River Podencos

In April 2011 a very emaciated Podenco was found in a storm drain next to the River Guadalquivir. She was nursing her puppies, and desperate for help. The weather was unseasonably wet, and there was a real danger that this family would be drowned in the rising water levels. A Spanish rescue centre in Seville, which we work closely with, managed to rescue the dogs and placed them in a kennels to recover. It would have been almost impossible to rehome the animals in Spain, as they are so common, and so, by the time they had been in the kennels for almost a

continued page 90

86

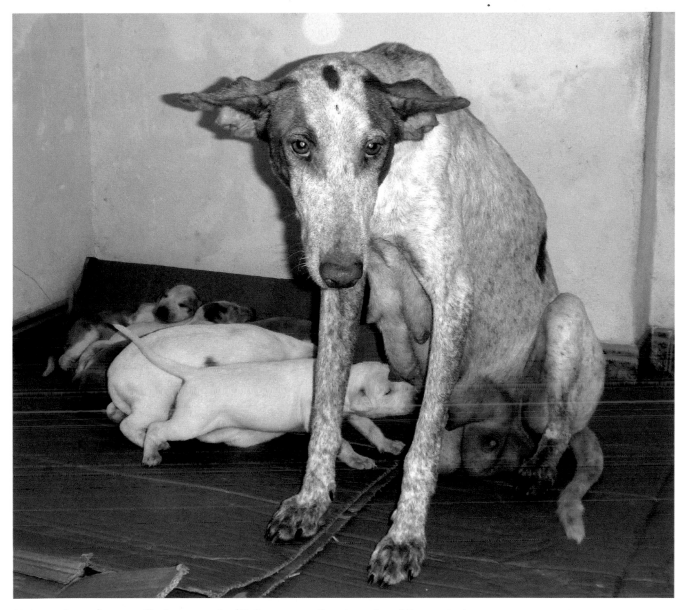

Betsy, when she was first rescued with her pups. (Courtesy Paqui Fernandez)

Overleaf – left: Stunning Guadiamar in foster care with us.

Overleaf – right: Huéznar exploring the British coast. (Courtesy Alex Smith)

year, We decided to take them onboard to try and find them homes.

The five puppies were each named after the tributaries that fed the River Guadalquivir, and Betsy is a rough translation of Guadalquivir. In the kennels the River Podenco family gradually recovered. The kennel environment was a safe and secure location, but the pups – a group of high energy, hunting stock hounds leaping around and loving their life – needed so much more in order to be satisfied and happy, frustrated by the necessary restrictions of shelter life.

First to come to the UK in 2012 were Betsy (who was probably a hunting dog who had escaped or been dumped), Genil and Viar. Betsy went into a foster home before being permanently rehomed in Basingstoke, Hampshire, and when her new family go on holiday she spends time back at her foster parents. Betsy loves the familiarity of these two wonderful homes, and is a calm and gentle girl who shows no sign of the horror she has lived through.

Genil was rehomed straight away to a family in Rugby, Warwickshire, who already had an SOS dog, and the two are very happy together. We found Viar her forever home in Kent, very near another SOS Podenco, and the pair regularly meet up for walks and doggy play dates.

A couple of months later Huéznar, Bembézar and Guadiamar came to England, with Huéznar going directly to her new home in Berkshire. This family already had a dog, and another family member has recently adopted a small terrier from us.

Bembézar went to a foster home in Bedfordshire, and the foster parents just could not let him go: another fabulous 'failed fosterer' who has fallen in love with a stunning Podenco.

Guadiamar came to us in Wales to be fostered, and it took us around two months to find her a home. A family in Herefordshire, whose daughter had previously taken a dog from us, fell in love with Guadiamar, and she now lives with their other dog in their lovely country house.

All five puppies are true Podencos: full of life, and loving nothing better than being able to charge around for hours on end. They are a stunning group of dogs with very unique coats and markings, like no other Podencos we have seen. None of these incredible dogs would have had any chance of finding a home in Spain, and would have been destined to life in a shelter had we not been made aware of their plight.

Sam and Ninja, the Galgos: two for the future …

During a recent trip to Spain two Galgos, found abandoned, were brought into one of our foster homes. It transpired that these two dogs had just arrived at another rescue centre, but because local hunters had been trying to steal dogs from the shelter, they were relocated for their safety. From the dogs' terrible condition it was obvious that they needed special care, so the pair were taken straight to a foster home.

Sam and Ninja were in the most appalling state and very close to death. Both dogs were so thin that their spines and ribs looked stretched over their skin, and both had open wounds and scars all over their bodies. Sam's tail will need to be amputated as it is so lacerated and severely infected from sitting in his own faeces and urine. Both dogs require round-the-clock care, and are fed frequent small meals to restore them to full health.

When I met them I was amazed at their fighting spirit, and how trusting they both are, and could see in these two beautiful boys the same fighting spirit that Micky had. It's still very early days for these lads, but both dogs are slowly getting there, making progress each day towards a full recovery. I am looking forward to finding these wonderful, gentle boys their own forever homes, and receiving the usual, always-welcome photo of them happy and warm on a sofa.

As you can tell, our work is always ongoing … but always rewarding.

Main: Sam

Inset: Ninja.

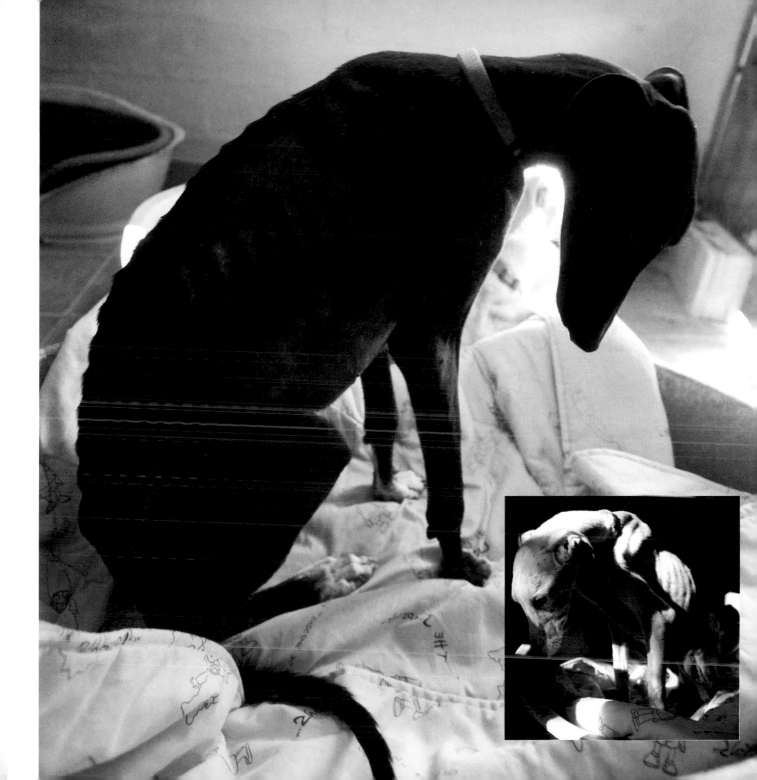

The truth ABOUT wolves & dogs

DISPELLING THE MYTHS OF DOG TRAINING

Hubble & Hattle

TONI SHELBOURNE

"Few people know wolves as well as they know dogs, and yet the link is both obvious, fascinating and important. This book reveals a lot we dog lovers should know" – Chris Packham (naturalist, nature photographer, television presenter and author)

"... very well illustrated ... many wonderful pictures of wolves and dogs" – Marc Bekoff (author, Professor Emeritus, University of Colorado)

Paperback • 250x250mm • 112 pages • 126 colour images • ISBN: 9781845844271 • £14.99*

5 STAR AMAZON REVIEWS –

"This visually stunning and beautifully written book eloquently explores the differences and similarities between wolves and dogs ... clarifies why the outdated and scientifically inaccurate 'dominance' methods are inappropriate and ultimately damaging to the very special human-canine bond"

"I've highly recommended [this book] to my clients, my canine psychology students, and my colleagues who work in the areas of dog behaviour and training"

"Well researched and written: this book does indeed make a valuable contribution to pulling the rug from under the feet of the dominance-based theories of dog training"

"All who love and work with dogs will find this volume a delight"

Tula